ARCHIE BRAIN

WOULD YOU RATHER
TRAVEL EDITION

Hilarious boredom busters for kids

MOUNTAINS

LAKE

GAME BOOK

HOW TO PLAY

Would You Rather is a game where you're faced with two silly or crazy choices, but you're only allowed to choose only one.

It's the perfect game for kids, teens and adults to play on a long car trip, plane journey or road trip!

You can ponder silly questions or make some challenging choices.

When faced with two equally difficult options, making a choice can feel impossible!

One person asks the question, everyone else can discuss their answer to question before choosing between them.

You might take minutes discussing your answer, or you could take hours!

There's only one rule in a 'Would you rather' game, and that is, have fun !

Are you ready?

Then, let's get started!

WOULD YOU RATHER ...

do cartwheels on the beach
and get sand in your eyes
OR dive into a lake
and get water up your nose?

stand on your head
for 15 minutes
OR run through the streets
shouting 'I'm a coconut!'?

WOULD YOU RATHER ...

be chauffeur-driven 5 miles in a gold Rolls Royce or take a 1000 mile roadtrip in a beat-up RV?

be rich and only have 3 weeks to live or be poor and have 3 years to live?

WOULD YOU RATHER ...

travel to Mars
in a Rocket
OR take a Road trip
to the Rocky Mountains?

travel to Hollywood to meet
your favorite movie star
OR travel to Jerusalem
to meet Jesus?

WOULD YOU RATHER ...

time travel
forward in time
or time travel
backwards in time?

live through
a zombie apocalypse
or live through
the French Revolution?

WOULD YOU RATHER ...

build a house
out of Lego
OR build a house
out of straw?

be thrown into
a pit of snakes
OR be thrown into
a den of lions?

WOULD YOU RATHER ...

someone read your
secret diary
or that someone watched
you on a secret camera?

go to a theme park and
only go on one ride
or go to the zoo and
be able to feed the lions?

WOULD YOU RATHER ...

feel
too hot
OR feel
too cold?

be the post boy who rises
to be company chairman OR
the accountant who stays in
the same job for 30 years?

WOULD YOU RATHER ...

go down the world's
longest water slide
OR go on the world's
scariest rollercoaster?

have no
mobile phone
OR have
no chocolate or candy?

WOULD YOU RATHER ...

be Neil Armstrong and
travel to the moon
or be Roald Amundsen and
travel to the South Pole?

meet the President
at White House
or visit the Queen
at Buckingham Palace?

WOULD YOU RATHER ...

wake up
as a Rabbit
OR wake up
as a guineapig?

drive
a tractor
OR drive
a petrol tanker?

WOULD YOU RATHER ...

work hard
and retire at age 40
or take it easy
and retire at age 65?

live in a 6-bedroom mansion
with a leaky roof or
live in a 2-bedroom cottage
with all expenses paid for?

15

WOULD YOU RATHER ...

be as strong
as a lion
or be as fast
as a gazelle?

have a cockroach
fall on your head
or wake up to find a huge
spider on your face?

WOULD YOU RATHER ...

travel in time to
meet Abraham Lincoln
OR travel in time to meet
Winston Churchill?

eat birds nest soup
in China
OR eat escamole (fried ant
larvae) in Mexico?

WOULD YOU RATHER ...

travel in time to see the Declaration of Independence signed or see Guy Fawkes try to set fire to the Houses of Parliament?

be only a tenth of your current height or be ten times your current height?

WOULD YOU RATHER ...

get up a 5am
every day
or stay up to
midnight every night?

sit in a bath
of cold porridge
or sit in a bath
or cold custard?

WOULD YOU RATHER ...

lie in front of a charging
herd of elephants
or stand in front of a
raging bull?

have to tell one lie
every day
or have to tell the truth
every day?

WOULD YOU RATHER ...

turn into
a kangaroo
or turn into
a koala bear?

travel by foot to the
top of a mouintain
or travel in a submarine
to the bottom of the sea?

WOULD YOU RATHER ...

have to
give up eating chocolate
OR have to give up
eating meat?

live with
a pink unicorn
OR live with
a purple gorilla?

WOULD YOU RATHER ...

wake up to discover
you're a mermaid
or wake up to discover
you're a unicorn?

be photographed naked
on the beach
or be photographed
naked around your home?

WOULD YOU RATHER ...

live in a log cabin
in the forest
or live in a straw shack
by the ocean?

be an astronaut
exploring far off galaxies
or be the first person to
live on the planet Mars?

WOULD YOU RATHER ...

be able to lift
any weight
OR be able to
jump any height?

be able to speak
5 different languages
OR be able to own
5 different cars?

WOULD YOU RATHER ...

feel everything
too much
or never feel
anything at all?

meet a famous baseball
player from the past
or meet a famous tennis
player from the past?

WOULD YOU RATHER ...

put your head inside
a lion's mouth
or run across
burning coals?

learn to fly
a plane
or learn to
pilot a cruise ship?

WOULD YOU RATHER ...

win the
Nobel Peace Prize
or win an Oscar for
best actor/actress?

walk through
the back streets of Paris
or trek through the
heart of the jungle?

WOULD YOU RATHER ...

be
a ballet dancer
or be
a cheer leader?

win an Olympic Gold Medal
for Rowing
or win an Olympic Gold Medal
for volleyball?

WOULD YOU RATHER ...

be chased by an
angry polar bear
or be chased by a swarm
of angry bees?

be an
only child
or have an older brother
who always picks on you?

WOULD YOU RATHER ...

be
Zac Efron
or be
Tom Hanks?

be
Marilyn Monroe
or be
Audrey Hepburn?

WOULD YOU RATHER ...

find a hoard of
buried treasure
or discover a way to
cure a terrible disease?

go on vacation
four times each year, or
have an unlimited amount of
money to spend on clothes?

WOULD YOU RATHER ...

meet
the Easter Bunny
OR meet the
Tooth Fairy?

they passed a law
to make chocolate illegal
OR that they passed a law
to make baseball illegal?

WOULD YOU RATHER ...

drive a
fire truck
or drive
an ambulance?

wake up to find your body
covered in mosquitoes
or wake up to find your
body covered in ants ?

WOULD YOU RATHER ...

have be
super-strong
or be
super-fast?

kiss
a frog
or kiss
a stranger?

WOULD YOU RATHER ...

go camping in the Rain in the summer
or go camping in the sun in the winter?

be known for walking the length of the Amazon River or be known for climbing to the top of Everest?

WOULD YOU RATHER ...

be very rich,
but stupid,
or be very poor,
but smart?

swim with
bottlenose dolphins
or swim with
megamouth sharks?

WOULD YOU RATHER ...

be the most
awkward person
or be the
biggest geek?

it was Christmas
every day
or that it was your
birthday every day?

WOULD YOU RATHER ...

turn everything
you touch into gold
or turn everything
you touch into chocolate?

eat a red hot
chilli pepper
or have to hold 10 ice cubes
in your mouth for 5 minutes?

WOULD YOU RATHER ...

Ride a
huge frog
or ride a
tiny dinosaur?

soar high
as an eagle
or dive deep
as a sperm whale?

WOULD YOU RATHER ...

live in a dark, dingy basement
OR live in a
cold, isolated loft?

be three
years younger
OR be three
years older?

WOULD YOU RATHER ...

be missing
one leg
or be blind
in one eye?

die in
an alien invasion
or work as a slave
for the alien invaders?

WOULD YOU RATHER ...

wake up with the ears of an elephant OR wake up with the ears of a giraffe?

have a fairy godmother who grants your wish once a year or have a genie who grants you 3 wishes now?

WOULD YOU RATHER ...

be able to read
people's minds
or be able to understand
animals minds?

watch seven movies
back to back
or watch an entire season
of your favorite show?

WOULD YOU RATHER ...

be allergic
to all animals
or be allergic
to dairy?

zoom along the world's
longest zip line
or jump off the world's
highest bungee jump?

WOULD YOU RATHER ...

play hide and seek
with a hippo
OR play baseball
with a lion?

swim in a
cRocodile-infested RIVER
OR hike through a
lio-infested jungle?

WOULD YOU RATHER ...

never eat another
ice cream
or never eat another
burger?

be remembered
for being generous
or be remembered
for being clever?

WOULD YOU RATHER ...

have a hot tub that's big enough for 12 friends or have a swimming pool that's big enough for 2?

have a
third nipple
or have two
belly buttons?

WOULD YOU RATHER ...

live in the time of
the Romans
OR live in the
time of the Vikings?

be painted purple
from top to bottom
OR have your
face tattooed?

WOULD YOU RATHER ...

forget the nasty things someone said to you or keep thinking about them for days?

have a tummy that's constantly rumbling or have a problem with constantly farting?

WOULD YOU RATHER ...

be captain of
a space shuttle
OR be captain of
a pirate ship?

accept your knighthood (OR
damehood) at Buckingham
Palace wearing a pink tutu
OR a purple feather boa?

WOULD YOU RATHER ...

be homeless for
a week
or away from your family
for a month?

eat only pizza
for a month
or eat only vegetables
for a month?

WOULD YOU RATHER ...

give up your computer
for a week
or give up social media
for a month?

fly 10,000 miles to see
somewhere new
or drive 10 miles to see
somewhere familiar?

WOULD YOU RATHER ...

climb up
a tree
or swing between two trees
in a hammock?

be
Prince Harry
or be
Prince William?

WOULD YOU RATHER ...

eat half a kilo
of raw liver
or eat half a kilo
of raw onions?

be the
most popular person
or be the
smartest person?

WOULD YOU RATHER ...

have a million followers
on social media
or have a million
in the bank?

become
rich and famous
or become
the happiest person alive?

WOULD YOU RATHER ...

be mistaken for your
mother's sister
or be mistaken for
your sister's mother?

be hung upside down
by your toenails or
hang over a precipice holding
on by your fingernails?

WOULD YOU RATHER ...

eat a
Rotten apple
OR swallow
a Rotten egg?

have Rich paRents who gave
you money, but not time, oR
have pooR paRents who gave
you time, but not money?

WOULD YOU RATHER ...

always have
smelly breath
or always have
stinky feet?

be Irish
living in America
or be American
living in Ireland?

WOULD YOU RATHER ...

dance in front of an
audience of 1000 people
OR sing in front of an
audience of 10,000 people?

star in your own
TV show
OR be an extra in
your favorite movie

WOULD YOU RATHER ...

be lost
in a snowstorm
OR be lost
in a strange city?

help with
the cooking
OR help with
the washing up?

WOULD YOU RATHER ...

write
amazing stories
or painting
incredible paintings?

win a free ticket
to a theme park
or win a free ticket
to a sports game?

WOULD YOU RATHER ...

have an endless supply
of ice cream
or an endless supply
of chocolate and candy?

cure every sickness in
the world
or feed everyone in the
world that's hungry?

WOULD YOU RATHER ...

be able to live anywhere in the world you choose or be able to have as many pets as you like?

arrive at the party overdressed or arrive at the party underdressed?

WOULD YOU RATHER ...

always be
ten minutes late
or always be
ten minutes early?

walk for
five miles
or swim for
500 metres?

WOULD YOU RATHER ...

spend a year helping out
at an orphanage
or spend a year helping out
at a prison?

turn into
a dragon
or turn into
a zombie?

WOULD YOU RATHER ...

have your bedroom
filled with pingpong balls
or have your bedroom
filled with foam?

be great with
words and speeches
or be great with
money and investments?

WOULD YOU RATHER ...

be able to watch any movie
at double the speed
OR be able to type
at twice the speed?

be an amazing singer,
but look very ordinary,
OR look amazing,
but be unable to sing?

WOULD YOU RATHER ...

eat sushi
in Japan
or eat raw fish
in Scandinavia?

be president of
the United States
or run a charity that feeds
thousands of children?

WOULD YOU RATHER ...

be a famous
baseball player
OR be the coach behind
a famous baseball team?

be POOR,
but loved,
OR be Rich
and live alone?

WOULD YOU RATHER ...

never be able to
sneeze again
OR never be able to
scRatch an itch again?

be have gReen slime
pouRed oveR you
OR have cold jelly/jello
pouRed oveR you?

WOULD YOU RATHER ...

be really good at Math,
but awful at spelling,
or be a spelling genius,
but awful at Math?

have everything
you think become true
or have everything
you say become true?

WOULD YOU RATHER ...

be so sick you have to stick your head in a bucket for a week or be so sick you have to sit on the toilet for a week?

be up all night with a crying baby or be up all night waiting for a new baby to arrive?

WOULD YOU RATHER ...

only be able
to whisper
OR only be able
to shout?

always REMEMBER
everything you see and hear
OR be able to choose to
forget some memories?

WOULD YOU RATHER ...

have your
eyebrows tweezed
or have your
legs waxed?

be
Sherlock Holmes
or be
Hercules Poirot?

WOULD YOU RATHER ...

tRavel in time to
sail on a Viking ship
oR tRavel in time to watch
a gladiatoR fight in Rome?

be woRld famous
foR being Rich
oR be woRld famous
foR bReaking a woRld RecoRd?

WOULD YOU RATHER ...

be able to shoot
fire from your fingertips
or be able to shoot lightning
bolts with your eyes?

have invented
the airplane
or have invented
the internet?

WOULD YOU RATHER ...

live in a tumbledown
shack for a month
or stay in a prison cell
overnight?

have an embarrassing
sounding laugh
or have an embarrassing
farting problem?

WOULD YOU RATHER ...

have a
pet Rat
oR have a
pet goldfish?

be known foR
stopping climate change
oR be known foR
stopping plastic pollution?

WOULD YOU RATHER ...

eat
a worm
or eat
a wasp?

be a
martial arts ninja
or be a
really good doctor?

WOULD YOU RATHER ...

eat only chicken
for a year
or eat only beeef
for a year?

visit five museums
and/or art galleries,
or go to the movies
just once?

WOULD YOU RATHER ...

be an owl
living high up in a tree
or be a fox
prowling the forest floor?

take a cruise ship
to China
or fly to China
by the fastest route?

WOULD YOU RATHER ...

eat guinea pig in Peru
or eat Rocky Mountain
oyster (fried bull testicles)
in the United States?

live in a house
with no power,
or live in a house,
with no running water?

WOULD YOU RATHER ...

go for a year
without sugar
or go for a year
without fruit?

be able to travel
anywhere in time
or be able to teleport
anywhere in the world?

WOULD YOU RATHER ...

live in a big city
and never see trees
or live in a forest cabin
and never see people?

have the
memory of an elephant
or have the
height of a giraffe?

WOULD YOU RATHER ...

paraglide out of
a small plane
or bungee jump
from a tall bridge?

live in a
small house in a big city
or live in a big house
in a small town?

WOULD YOU RATHER ...

travel in time
to meet Nelson Mandela
OR travel in time to meet
President John F Kennedy?

have to run
to catch a plane
OR have to run
to catch a thief?

WOULD YOU RATHER ...

have Count Dracula
take you out to dinner
or have King Kong
take you out to dinner?

win 5000
as a prize
or have your best friend
win 500,000 as a prize?

WOULD YOU RATHER ...

endure the sting of doing a
belly flop in the pool
OR endure the pain of
stubbing your toe?

be tickled until you
can barely breath
OR tickle someone until they
can barely breath?

WOULD YOU RATHER ...

eat a jelly bean that tastes like grandad's earwax or eat a jelly bean that tastes of dog slobber?

be the World Record holder for having the most skin piercings or for having the longest toenails?

WRITE YOUR OWN ...

If you've had fun with these 'Would You Rather' questions (and even if you haven't!), making up your own questions can be fun.

Why not get creative and write a few of your own over the following pages?

WRITE YOUR OWN WOULD YOU RATHER ...

?

?

WRITE YOUR OWN WOULD YOU RATHER ...

?

?

WRITE YOUR OWN WOULD YOU RATHER ...

?

?

WRITE YOUR OWN
WOULD YOU RATHER ...

?

?

WRITE YOUR OWN
WOULD YOU RATHER ...

?

?

WRITE YOUR OWN
WOULD YOU RATHER ...

?

?

WRITE YOUR OWN
WOULD YOU RATHER ...

?

?

WOULD YOU RATHER ...

Other books by Archie Brain include:

<u>Would You Rather - Travel Edition</u> - makes a great boredom buster for long car rides, road trips or plane journeys.

It's filled with silly and fun questions to ask your family and friends!

Coming soon:

Would You Rather Easter Edition

Would You Rather Disgusting & Gross Edition

Would You Rather Zombie Apocalypse Edition

Follow Archie Brain on Amazon to be notified of new releases!